I0415027

Imagine a car that has been in an accident. It is structurally unsound, but can be soldered up to look roadworthy. It's patched up and put back on the road. But at the first test of strength, it falls apart. That is what a narcissistic man is like-he may look 'roadworthy' but it's all an act. He too will fall apart at the first test of strength. And where does that leave you? Stranded by the road with a clapped out piece of junk.

Copyright © Nikki Asquith. All rights reserved. Permission must be obtained to reproduce whole or part of this publication. Extracts reproduced with permission.

Disclaimer:

Except where quoting from other sources, the contents of this book are the honest opinion of the author. The information in this book does not constitute professional advice. Everyone's situation is unique, and you must make your own decisions based on your particular circumstances.

The author makes no warranty with regard to the accuracy of the resources or references contained herein and will not be liable for any errors or omissions.

Fictitious names and scenarios have been used in the case studies presented throughout this book, for illustrative purposes. Any resemblance to persons, alive or dead, or circumstances is purely coincidental.

In no event shall the author be liable for any damages, injury or other outcomes arising from the use or performance of the information in this book.

Index

Introduction

For every woman who identifies her partner as a narcissist and deals with him effectively, there are countless more that are still in the dark about their relationship. They may feel very hurt, confused and ashamed at the way their partner behaves towards them. They may want to seek help, but don't know where or how to start. Or they may have tried talking to someone about it, but not received the understanding and support they needed. In the meantime, their narcissistic partner is whittling away their confidence, happiness and peace of mind, and once he is finished, he leaves with another unsuspecting victim.

I think the narcissistic men of this world have it far too easy because most women have no idea what they are dealing with when they come across a narcissistic man. Time to change that power imbalance- and what better way to do it than to give women some tools to identify and deal with a narcissist. Practical tips such as what works and what doesn't; the best places to go for help; tips for family and friends; and some cheeky ways to get back at a narcissistic partner!

It is possible to survive and triumph over the experience of a narcissistic partner when you know what you are dealing with, and how to deal with it. It is my hope that by using the tools in this book, women can move towards a fulfilling relationship and far, far away from a narcissistic man!

Remember: the best revenge is a wonderful life-which is something a narcissist will never have.

1. What is a narcissist?

A narcissist is someone who displays some or all of the traits of Narcissistic Personality Disorder (NPD) to varying degrees. NPD is rarely diagnosed because narcissists aren't likely to admit they have a problem or seek help. Diagnosing NPD is also difficult to do, even for trained professionals; but there seems little point diagnosing it anyway as there is a low success rate in treating NPD.

What is NPD?

Five of the following criteria must be met for NPD to be diagnosed[1]:

❖ The person feels grandiose and self-important (e.g. exaggerates accomplishments, talents, skills, contacts and personality traits to the point of lying; demands to be recognised as superior without commensurate achievements).

❖ The individual is obsessed with fantasies of unlimited success, fame, fearsome power or omnipotence, unequalled brilliance (the *cerebral narcissist*), bodily beauty or sexual

---

[1] I refer here to Sam Vaknin's amended American Psychiatric Association *Diagnostic and Statistical Manual of Mental Disorders,* 4th ed., USA, 1994 (DSM-IV) criteria, as I feel they cover more aspects of NPD behaviour than others I have read. Vaknin Dr S., *Malignant Self Love — Narcissism revisited,* 1st ed. 8th revision, Narcissism Publications, Prague and Skopje, 2007, p. 33.

performance (the *somatic narcissist*); or ideal, everlasting, all-conquering love or passion.

❖ They are firmly convinced that he or she is unique and, being special, can only be understood by, should only be treated by, or associate with, other special, or unique, or high-status people (or institutions).

❖ The person requires excessive admiration, adulation, attention and affirmation or, failing that, wishes to be feared and to be notorious (*Narcissistic Supply*).

❖ They feel entitled: they demand automatic and full compliance with his or her unreasonable expectations for special and favourable priority treatment.

❖ The individual is "interpersonally exploitative", i.e. uses others to achieve his or her own ends.

❖ They are devoid of empathy: unable or unwilling to identify with, acknowledge, or accept the feelings, needs, preferences, priorities and choices of others.

❖ The person is constantly envious of others and seeks to hurt or destroy the objects of his or her frustration; suffers from persecutory (paranoid) delusions as he or she believes that others feel the same about him or her and are likely to act similarly.

❖ They behave arrogantly and haughtily: feel superior, omnipotent, omniscient, invincible, immune, "above the law", and omnipresent (magical thinking). They rage when frustrated, contradicted, or confronted by people he or she considers inferior to him or her and unworthy.

Between 50-75% of those diagnosed with NPD are males.[2]

---

[2] American Psychiatric Association *Diagnostic and Statistical Manual of Mental Disorders,* 4th ed., USA, 1994

2. Narcissistic hallmarks

Narcissistic Supply is their drug of choice

To paraphrase Dr Sam Vaknin's excellent explanation — a narcissist (N) is focused on securing attention. He does this by creating and projecting a "fake" self to the world and gauges the reactions of others to this "new" self. What he[3] is looking for is the attention he gets from others in response to his mask. This attention, or *Narcissistic Supply* (NS), is his *raison d'etre*; this is not a "nice to have" — it is as essential as oxygen. It drives everything he does.

Sources of NS

A narcissist looks for people who will give him NS.

To work out your partner's source of NS, take a look at:

❖ What he spends most of his time doing

❖ What it is that has been eluding him? Listen to his history. Is it happiness in a family, a relationship? Or is it success in a career?

❖ Who he does favours for (i.e. who is he trying to impress?)

---

[3] This book was written for women dealing with a narcissistic male partner, which is why I use male references throughout. The content may equally apply to female narcissists.

❖ Who he emulates, for example, buying the same things, going to the same places, dressing the same.

This can be a little tricky as his source of NS is likely to have changed over time: just because his friends were his source of NS in his 20's does not mean that his current friends are his source of NS now.

Also, there may be multiple sources of NS in varying degrees. For example, Gigi could never understand why her partner preferred to be with his drinking buddies rather than her. This was because they were his primary source of attention and she was a secondary source — a trophy girlfriend.

Pedestal aerobics — value/devalue

The narcissist puts those who give him NS on a pedestal, but as he inevitably gets bored or finds fault with them, he brings them down to his level[4]. What he is trying to do is cause you to feel as bad he does behind his false self.

This is what is so confusing, emotionally and psychologically. One minute you are the best looking girl in the state, the next he is making comments such as, "You could make an effort to look nice for me" when you are sick with the flu! It's like being bitten by a mosquito — you feel it, think it's a one-off and you are safe from further bites. Then you get zapped again.

N's are very good at making you believe their behaviour is somehow your fault — that you misunderstood them or are

---

[4] Vaknin Dr S., *Malignant Self Love,* p. 121.

being too sensitive. They also punish you severely for the most minor transgressions: you are left in no doubt that you will be disposed of if you upset them, and since you love them and want to be with them, being ignored is torture. So you learn to avoid that by saying little or nothing. For example, Mary tried calling her N after she had a car accident; he didn't answer or return her call. Later that night, she told him why she had called and explained that she was upset he didn't call back. N's response was to disappear. What she didn't know was he had started seeing someone else and was trying to get out of their relationship.

N's are also experts at minimising what happened, denying anything happened at all, or refusing to discuss it — as if not acknowledging it means it doesn't exist!

Hall of mirrors

A narcissist is a hall of mirrors reflecting what he thinks others want to see, so you will never get consistency or intimacy. One minute he says he likes something, a month later he says he doesn't. For example, Jennifer's N used to be desperate to go to Hawaii. When she talked about organising a holiday there a few years later, he criticised the idea. It was a complete 180 degree turn on his former position. When she reminded him how he used to want to go he just blandly noted, "Oh yeah".

It's tiring being with someone who is always moving the goal posts. It's no good for your mental health either.

You are also a reflection of what your N partner wants you to be, so he won't be seeing you as you truly are. He will assume what you like, want and need and won't listen to your actual wishes. This means you don't ever get what you want — and he doesn't really care what you want anyway. A good relationship involves developing an understanding of each other *as you are,* not pretending your partner is someone else, which is exactly what a narcissist does.

Lying

Narcissists can't help themselves, it's like a game of "catch me if you can": they lie constantly about all sorts of things. One reason is that N's don't want to be "discovered" — they consider they are far too complex and special to be understood by anyone. They also adjust their performance for the audience they are seeking NS from.

A classic example of this behaviour is when your N partner denies a particular conversation took place; another is saying that he will call, then not doing so. If you raise it with him he may deny ever saying he would call; or voice some other reality-vortex classic like: "Oh, what I meant was that *you should call me*". They won't do the things they say they will, because they have no intention of following through — they are just telling you what they know you want to hear. They will also keep things from you (lying by omission).

For example, Terry answered the phone one evening and took a message for her N partner. It was a friend of her N's calling to congratulate him on his recent performance in a local theatre production. When her N partner arrived home, she asked him about the role and why he didn't tell her about it. At first he refused to tell her; then he said he was doing someone a favour.

Terry's N was constantly claiming to be too busy with work to help at home since their first child arrived, so she was furious. Terry later discovered that her N partner had been participating in theatre productions since they learnt of her pregnancy, and had invited his co-workers along to some of his performances. Meanwhile, Terry had no idea! He said he lied because he wanted to "see how it went" and invite her "when he could be proud of his performance" — Terry thought that sounded plausible.

The "plausible" lie is a narcissistic hallmark; but over time there are many "plausible" lies and purported "misunderstandings". It is a pattern, and the reasons behind these "plausible" lies stop being relevant.

When caught out in a lie, a narcissist either doesn't care, won't respond, or will make out you are mistaken. This latter behaviour falls into the next category.

Gaslighting

In the movie "Gaslight", a man tries to convince his wife that she is going crazy by manipulating aspects of her physical environment and denying things were as she correctly recalled them. For example, every night he secretly goes into the attic; when he turns on the lights in the attic, the gaslights in the rooms below flicker. The wife notices this but her husband tries to make her believe she is imagining it. Hence the term: Gaslighting.

Karla's N partner was great at doing this; mainly by denying conversations had taken place or plans had been made. For example, he told her he would cook dinner for her for Valentines Day. Come the 14th of February, Karla got dressed up for dinner. 7pm-but no N. She tried calling his cell phone but it was switched off. He arrived at 9pm with take-away food. When she asked him what had happened and reminded him about his plan to cook her dinner he replied, "No, I never said that", totally deadpan, as if she had imagined the whole thing. He later admitted that he had said he would cook her a Valentines Day dinner. Another time he told her that "her feelings were unreasonable" when he did something to upset her. This really perplexed her — she felt like she was in the wrong for being hurt by his actions.

When Barbara's N was arrested for drink driving, he told her she shouldn't put up with it. Yet when she did get mad at him, he got upset!

I believe N's actually derive a sick sense of pleasure from testing their partners to see what they can get you to believe, and whether they can upset you or not. A lot of times you may know your N is messing you around, but you don't have the energy to pull them up on it.

Pressing your buttons

As master manipulators, narcissists are excellent at pressing your buttons: they will mercilessly do the things that drive you to distraction to make you react in a certain way, all so they can bring you down. For example, Alice's N partner knew she hated it when he ignored her, so he would go AWOL, not answer messages, and not call or see her for days (classic abusive behaviour, by the way!). Alice would get more and more upset. Her partner would take his sweet time to get back to her and, when he did, he would be completely calm and unflustered as if nothing had happened. Alice would then be at boiling point and let him have it, but he would play the innocent — "where did this come from?"— which made Alice look like the out-of-control, crazy girlfriend. That suited him perfectly because he had successfully taken Alice's focus from the original issue. In the process, he brought the power back to himself and put Alice in the position of being in the wrong!

This ability to control you like a puppet is something an N derives pleasure from. He gets to look down on this person who can't control their emotions, which makes him feel that much more in control of his. Your behaviour also gives him justification (in his view) for treating you badly.

Public versus private persona

The N is very much like Jekyll and Hyde: Dr Jekyll being the mild mannered doctor and public face; Mr Hyde the violent monster who murdered prostitutes by night. You may wonder why your partner is so nice to complete strangers, work colleagues, family and friends, and why you bear the worst of his behaviour. This dramatic difference is really a form of Gaslighting, in my view.

Publicly, Vera's N partner was sociable and entertaining, but he rarely showed this side with her. He would go out with friends and work colleagues, but she was lucky to be invited along once a year. Vera was expected to be sitting at home waiting for him to arrive, and if she wasn't home when he did arrive, then he panicked! That is exactly what happened when Vera was not home when he called by one Friday evening: her N rang her on her mobile to check where she was — he was worried she had gone away and not told him about it. The shoe didn't fit on the other foot very well!

Lack of empathy

What is empathy? It's the ability to step inside someone else's shoes — to have some understanding of what another person is experiencing or feeling.

N's can't empathise, but they have learnt what sort of behaviour to assume, in situations where empathy is expected, in order to secure NS[5]. This NS can be adulation for being so supportive (positive ego reinforcement), to the other end of the spectrum such as keeping you from getting angry at them for not being supportive (avoiding damage to their ego). Their brand of "empathy" is all about them, however, and not you.

For example, one night Sally burnt her hand badly while ironing his work shirt. N's response was, "Oh, a burn", then he proceeded to eat his dinner in front of the TV! Sally was in too much pain to react.

Jessica agreed to let some of her N's friends from interstate stay at their house. Jessica had broken her arm, so she told her N that her agreement was conditional on her N helping to prepare the house for their visitors. The night before they arrived, her N still had not helped clean the house, prepare the guest room or do the shopping. When she confronted him

---

[5] Vaknin Dr S., *Malignant Self Love*, p. 124.

18

about it, all he said was "do it yourself". Jessica was stunned. She had to call a cleaning service the next day and get her N partner to stall their arrival.

Avoiding joint social activities

Your N partner may rarely spend time socially with you. This is usually done to avoid people he feels inferior to, and to avoid having his behaviour towards you being publicly displayed. Also, it's his way of controlling your desire to be with him: the more you complain, or the more people ask about that elusive boyfriend of yours, the more special he feels. Alternatively, you may not be his primary source of NS, so he isn't going to be putting the effort into your joint social activities.

Nara's N refused to attend a party with her because he was busy cleaning his oven (on a Saturday night?). He refused to spend the holidays with her; he also planned to work rather than attend her graduation party. You get the picture.

Intimidation into isolation

This process starts out with your N partner not confirming a time to see you, or not being interested in going to social events with you, so you end up cancelling arrangements you have made to spend time with him. You also want to avoid the stigma of having a "bad relationship", so you hide at home when he won't attend functions with you. Slowly people stop making plans with you on the weekends, and you are left waiting for him to appear, which he will do if and when he pleases. If you complain he will either ignore it or create such a fuss you regret even saying it.

By doing this he makes you ripe for further, unfettered and unmonitored abuse as there is no external feedback regarding the way he treats you.

A one-off doesn't count

Most people exhibit some form of narcissistic behaviour at some time or other. What you are looking for, though, is someone who exhibits some or all of these behaviours consistently. In other words, you are looking for a substantiated behavioural pattern.

3. Narcissistic abuse

You may wonder why you feel so terrible in your relationship, but can't really point to the reasons for it. You may not think what you are experiencing is serious enough to be considered abusive.

What is abuse?

Abuse includes the following behaviours displayed by a narcissist[6]:

❖ Unpredictable, inconsistent and irrational behaviour

❖ Disproportionate reactions

❖ Dehumanising

❖ Gaslighting

❖ Indifference and the silent treatment.

Still not convinced?

The definition of abuse is a grey area. There are some helpful resources in the last chapter of this book that you might want to look at to determine if your relationship is abusive. I suggest that you don't get too worried about whether something can be defined as abuse or not, it is a subjective test anyway. What

---

[6] Vaknin Dr S., *Toxic Relationships — Abuse and its aftermath*, 4th ed., Narcissus Publications, Prague and Skopje 2007, pp. 13-18.

matters is what *you* felt about the behaviour and the circumstances. For instance, if your partner yelled at you to get out of the way when you were at risk of being run over by a truck, the situation would justify you being yelled at as he was saving you from harm.

The following are good indicators of an abusive narcissistic relationship:

❖ You are on an emotional rollercoaster

❖ You are in a "fog" because of the mind games or lies of your partner

❖ No matter what you say or do, it makes no difference to the way your partner treats you

❖ It's all about what your partner wants

❖ You are scared of the reactions of your partner.

Does this apply to me?

If your reaction to what you have read so far is, "Well, that doesn't apply to me!" there are two possibilities. The first, you aren't with a narcissist. Lucky you! The second is that you may be with a narcissist, but are unwilling or unable to admit it. That is OK; you will deal with things in your own way, and in your own time. You may wish to keep this book just in case your circumstances change.

Why don't you just kick him to the kerb?

If you have talked to your friends they may have given you well-meaning advice such as, "Don't take that crap! Stand up to him!", or, "Just leave him. You can do better!" If you are with an N partner, though, this advice just doesn't help. Why?

To start with, the valuing and devaluing cycle dents your confidence. You wonder why his behaviour has changed towards you and why he is so nice to others but not to you.

You may also be ashamed of what is happening and don't want it to become publicly known. Or you may not want to admit the reality of the situation, refusing to acknowledge his bad behaviour or just explaining it away — this is called "cognitive dissonance".

You are also likely to be experiencing Stockholm syndrome, where you cover up for your N partner and cut ties with those who criticise him or the relationship. You may avoid social situations where you know people will ask why he isn't with you or who question you about the way he treats you.

Rest assured it's a normal reaction to your situation.

Is this what you really want?

There is a proverb that says: "Love makes an effort. Indifference makes an excuse". If you are with an N you will get a lot of excuses. But what effort does he make?

Think carefully about how much time you spend thinking about and doing things to improve the relationship. Now, how much time is your partner spending on the relationship? And how seriously is he taking it? Does he consider your needs and wants? Does he walk the talk, or just placate you with sweet words?

Then, think about what you give to him. It's likely to be a lot more than he gives you, and way more than he deserves!

At the end of the day it's your life. But how much of it do you want to spend on someone who hurts you over and over again, who does not care about your feelings and who isn't there for you when you need them? How much time do you want to spend on someone who cheats and lies? Don't you deserve someone who wants to be with you, someone who includes you in their world?

There is something else to consider: your health. An abusive relationship impacts on your emotional, psychological and physical well-being. Just because you may not be physically abused, this does not mean you are not being harmed.

I don't know!

If you need some help thinking through the issues, Blase Harris MD wrote a very good chapter on impaired lovers in his book, "How to get your lover back".[7] Dr Harris talks about the basic qualities needed to have a love relationship and the qualities that indicate a person doesn't have what it takes. Chapter 16 of

---

[7] Harris B. M.D., *How to get your lover back*, Dell Publishing, USA, 1989.

Dr Patricia Allen's book, "Getting to I Do"[8], also looks at why women become trapped in a bad relationship.[7]

There are also some checklists in the resources section which may be helpful in clarifying your thoughts on the relationship. I strongly suggest you take a look at these references to honestly assess whether this relationship is really what you want.

Some things to think about are:

❖ Do you feel supported by him?

❖ Do you feel happy most of the time?

❖ Do you feel like you can be honest with your partner about what you need from the relationship?

❖ Do you have the freedom to be yourself in this relationship? Or are you pretending to be the person your narcissist has moulded you into, just to keep the relationship? For instance, you may be feisty, but with him you may not speak up if he upsets you.

❖ Look at your past relationships. How does this one feel compared to those?

---

[8] Allen Dr P. and Harmon S., *Getting to "I do"*, Harper Collins, USA, 1994.

4. Leaving a narcissist

It is best to make out that you are leaving your narcissist because of something unrelated to him: the reason being, it's less likely to dent that super-size ego of his. N's turn nasty very quickly when you upset them, and being dumped by a source of NS is pretty upsetting to them!

For instance, Julie's N fiancée told her he wanted to cancel their engagement. Julie was distraught, but recovered herself enough to think clearly, and told him she would be consulting her lawyer about their joint property. She asked him to call her with the name of his lawyer so they could sort out the details. Weeks went by, and her N still had not called with his lawyer's details, despite saying he would. He ignored her messages and calls. What was happening was her N was upset that Julie was cutting the cord and not begging him to reconsider.

Julie's N called a month later, all cheery—as if nothing had happened. He asked her out to lunch-but Julie was all business, and asked him for the name of his lawyer. He began yelling at her, saying she had no right to the property (it was in both their names)! Julie replied calmly that if he didn't want to use a lawyer she would have the legal documents delivered directly to him.

This anger arose because Julie's neutral approach was denying him NS. He was trying to pick a fight to get Julie to lose her cool and get some negative NS, but it wasn't working!

Please be aware that a narcissist can turn violent since they feel they are immune to the consequences of their actions.[9] Even if you have never experienced this in the past, the dramatic behavioural changes they can exhibit make it a possibility. Therefore, if you must see them, make sure you are with someone else, in public, or on neutral ground.

Having the strength to go

You need to be emotionally ready. It took Madeleine one break up, followed by a reunion and engagement which he broke off with a public fight at her family's Christmas dinner to get to the point where she was emotionally ready to leave her ex.

Madeleine looked back over the years and saw how he had won her over with promises and sweet words, then started to back-peddle, always giving her just enough to keep her there. She realised that he truly didn't care what he did to her, so she chose to take care of herself rather than wasting any more time on someone who wouldn't, and couldn't, do the most basic things in a relationship.

Rest assured you can, and will, get to a similar point eventually; so do not beat yourself up if it takes, or took, a long time to break free.

---

[9] Vaknin Dr S., *Toxic Relationships*, p. 114.

5. Mistakes women make

Taking a traditional approach

You are dealing with someone who *cannot empathise* — so appealing to his emotions, which is a characteristic of many traditional approaches, isn't going to work. Also, the more you open up and tell him that something makes you unhappy, the madder he will get; after all, you are, in effect, *criticising him*. He will then begin the search for an easier source of NS.

This doesn't mean that there is something wrong with you or your approach; far from it — it's working too well! So don't lose heart and clam up in your next relationship. You are just on your way to being with someone more genuine and who actually wants to *relate* to you, rather than keeping you as a reflection of the image he is projecting.

Also, it has been established that abuse happens in intimate relationships in response to the threat of looming intimacy.[10] So trying to connect emotionally with your N partner will ultimately make him lash out at you. It's not really worth the effort then, is it?

Thinking he will change/be different with you

Patterns don't lie. Look at his past relationships. Listen to him. Has he changed any of his behaviours that lead to break ups or which caused problems before? He is likely to be quite open and state that he knows his failure to do *x, y,* or *z* was an

---

[10] Vaknin Dr S., *Toxic Relationships,* p. 81.

issue in his other relationships, but he won't change his ways regardless of the consequences. If you ask him to go to counselling with you he is unlikely to agree.

I also believe that N's get worse with age, particularly close to middle age. Laura saw a dramatic change in her N's behaviour as he approached 50; his N qualities became dominant and the Mr Hyde part of his personality appeared front and centre. Until this time there had been enough of the good qualities to make her doubt her misgivings and bad feelings.

Trying to keep him happy by walking on eggshells

Walking on eggshells only prolongs the relationship and does not stop your N partner from treating you badly, nor does it stop him from ultimately leaving you when he finds an easier source of NS.

Giving up your friends, hobbies

Focus on strategies to keep you accountable to the outside world — join an activity with a friend or go out and meet new people. Try and make regular social times with friends and not talk about the relationship; you may feel like cocooning at home, but this is unhealthy if done over the long term. And believe me; if you are in a narcissistic relationship you will be cocooning yourself for months or years! So please don't do yourself a disservice by locking yourself away. Remember, you have a lot to offer the world — your relationship is not the marker of your worth, your talents, beauty or interest to others. Don't let your narcissistic partner *intimidate you into isolation*.

Develop a barometer of normal behaviour to monitor your partner's actions against. Pay attention to your relationships with male co-workers and friends. Observe how other people, particularly men, treat you, their partners, and others. You may see that you are getting far better treatment from others than your N partner.

Finally, surround yourself with people and things that make you feel good to help offset the poisonous effects of the narcissistic abuse. The more time you spend with people outside the relationship, the better it is for you in the long term, irrespective of who you are with! It makes you a much more interesting person.

Not getting help

A word of caution: friends and family do not understand the uniqueness of a narcissistic relationship; they may also be very shocked and not want to deal with the reality of what is going on. They may try to minimise what is happening or somehow try and blame the situation on you. Adriana had people laugh about the fact she considered her partner to be a narcissist, and another mock her "pop-psychology". Shona was quizzed about why she didn't realise her ex was a narcissist earlier on, why did she stay, etc? She felt like she had to defend herself to these people and decided she was not going to waste her energy trying. She just never discussed it with them again.

Therefore, I recommend looking at the self-help tools listed at the end of this book, or talking to a trained professional who can help you understand what a narcissistic relationship is and give you some strategies to deal with it. At a minimum, they can help you shine a light onto what the issues are and you can work out your path from there.

Another valuable source of help is other women who have experienced narcissistic abuse. One option is to read the stories of other women via internet pages listed in the Resources section, or you can find a narcissistic abuse support group. If the idea of discussing your relationship with a group of strangers is daunting to you, be aware that it may take some time before you feel comfortable about this step. Once you accept that you have survived the experience of a narcissistic partner, you may want and need the support of others with similar experiences.

I do strongly suggest, however, that you pay attention to the comments friends and family make about changes in *your* behaviour. You may have had people say things to you like "You never used to be like this", and, "Are you happy?" You will know deep down that they are right, but are likely to be wasting your energy pretending that everything is fine. This is a sign that you are suffering far more than you realise, and are at a point where you should get help from a professional.

Staying in contact after a break up, or getting back together (where there is no joint property or kids)

Staying in contact is a guarantee that he will hurt you again and again. He is only interested in testing whether he still has what it takes to hook you in and make you want him again, and then he will start treating you badly as he begins to devalue you. These cycles can last for months, or years. Fran's ex spent two years messing her around like this.

Also, your N partner will resent your ability to cope without him. As a friend of Fran's commented, she had the poor taste not to fall apart after the break up — she thrived! He will also not participate in activities with your friends or activities that you started doing after you broke up with him. For example, Deborah's ex took a "tit for tat" approach and established his own networks, and he refused to let her into them. He then used that against her when he complained she didn't spend enough time with him!

Telling him he is a narcissist

If you break the news to your partner that he is a narcissist, he is unlikely to accept it or get help, and he might start looking for someone else to support his ego.

Besides, telling them what the problem is doesn't mean they will do anything about it. Zahni asked her ex to go to counselling with her and he flatly refused; if the relationship was important enough, he would have sought help to save it.

Not setting boundaries

Once your N partner ascertains that you will put up with his bad behaviour, the floodgates are open for more of the same and it is likely to get steadily worse. So you need to be very clear on the behaviour you will and won't accept, and what will happen if he engages in this behaviour.[11] Walking away and staying away is a good consequence — if you can stand it! For example, Mindy's N used to constantly swear. She disliked it and felt uncomfortable about it, so to draw a boundary in a fun way, she told him that she would fine him 2 dollars the next time he used bad language.

Maintaining boundaries with a narcissist isn't easy!

Narcissists have a way of manipulating you that makes you feel like a puppet in their hands. And they are like sharks — they can sense weaknesses in their prey. This makes it very tough to enforce boundaries. In the above example, Mindy's N did inevitably swear in her presence. She reminded him of the rule and his response was to darkly say, "Well, if that's how you want to be", and sulk. He knew this would frighten Mindy into letting it go, which she did.

You may also find you just get tired of taking them to task on their lies and behaviour.

---

[11] Dr Henry Cloud and Dr John Townsend have written an excellent book on this topic called *Boundaries in Dating*, Zondervan, USA, 2000. Chapters 15, 16 and 18, in particular, deal with this issue and are a good resource for any relationship.

6. What to do

If you are still with him

Focus on you and be gentle

Being in a relationship with an N is like moving through quicksand — the harder you struggle, the faster you sink. So instead of focusing so much on trying to understand your partner or the relationship, stop, and put all that energy into looking after yourself. Sadly, it will make no difference how much time and energy you put into the relationship. When the N finds another source of NS, you will be history, so you might as well spend all that time and energy on making yourself the best you can be and attracting people and events into your life that are good for you. Start getting out there and meeting new people, and if there are eligible men in that mix, so much the better! You may find that by doing this your N partner ends up exiting your life because you change. If so, congratulate yourself on building a great life despite having your N trying to drag you down to his level like a dead weight.

Otherwise, prepare for a bumpy road and be gentle with yourself. An enormous amount of your subconscious energy is directed at suppressing your unhappiness and the fight or flight feelings you experience constantly in a relationship like this. You may find you get sick, have no energy, or get easily emotional — it is completely normal under the circumstances. The question is: is this what you want your normality to be?

Stay independent

Do not live with your N partner, set up joint accounts, or rely on him for work. Your aim is to be able to extract yourself from the relationship at your choosing, with minimal consequences in your life. When your N abruptly ups and leaves, without warning or justification, it will then affect you far less. You will also need to have an independent support network to help you get through the difficult post break-up times.

Set boundaries — state the consequences of poor behaviour and stick to them!

Sam Vaknin suggests that you should match the N's behaviour[12] — for example, if he is yelling, yell right back. The intention is to show him you are not going to be bullied and to give you a bit of your power back. Another approach is to calmly, and at an appropriate time, state something like this:

"I didn't feel comfortable when you ... (yelled at me in the store/told me I was stupid). If it happens again, I will be walking away from you and won't speak to you again until you apologise."

In Sally's case, this approach caused her N partner to exit — stage left — for an easier source of NS.

All relationships need boundaries, but with a narcissist you will be patrolling those boundaries constantly. Basically, you will

---

[12] Vaknin Dr S., *Toxic Relationships*, p. 31.

be a parent for your N partner, and you don't know how long for, or even whether it will work, and whether it will give you the type of relationship you are looking for. Ask yourself: how much energy am I willing to devote to this person and get back what I am currently getting? Do I really want another child?

Has he cheated?

If you both want to maintain the relationship, make sure he is willing to commit to you exclusively and to be accountable to you for his whereabouts and his actions. Also, his actions need to match his words consistently to rebuild trust between you. Remember that N's are skilful liars and you need to keep your wits about you to protect yourself from getting hurt again.

Set the terms of the relationship

I suggest drawing up an agreement about what your partner will do to repair your trust, and what the relationship will look like for the first month. Consider things like: Will you just be dating? If so, will it be exclusively? Or will you be officially back together? How often will you see/speak to each other?

Be prepared for this to be a short-term solution. Unfortunately, an N partner is unlikely to keep up the façade of good deeds for long, or get locked into something that requires him to be accountable to you on an on-going basis.

STDs

Insist your N partner get tested for HIV/AIDS and other sexually transmitted diseases. Also, demand that you see the results on paper or are allowed to go with him to the doctor to receive the results. You may have seen the ladies who were infected with HIV knowingly by Philippe Padieu.[13] One of the women who asked him the results of his HIV test took his word that it was clear; unfortunately it was a lie and she is now paying the terrible price. And remember, narcissists lie to secure NS, so he won't hesitate to cover up any problems if he wants your attention. Your life and health is far too important not to be resolute on this point.

Some may say this is draconian, but if you do the wrong thing there is a price to pay. Ask yourself: if it was you who cheated, would you be willing to show your partner you were trustworthy to keep the relationship? Don't take any sanctimonious rubbish like, "I can't be with you if you don't trust me", either. Think about what *he* would do if the situation was reversed; and if your partner is squawking about privacy violations, ask yourself why? If he has nothing to hide, it shouldn't matter.

---

[13] For details of this story go to http://www.oprah.com/health/New-Faces-of-HIV-and-AIDS.

If you have broken up with him

Grief

You will grieve for many things — the lost relationship; the months or years you allowed him to mess you around; the dreams you shared that were just an illusion; and the fact that you were so callously discarded and easily replaced.

Grief is like waves. You will find you have hours/days/weeks where you feel OK, then something triggers a memory — the same cologne, for example — and you remember... you miss him... you wonder why this had to happen. You may even want him back; this is normal. The best way to handle it is to acknowledge how you are feeling. It will pass. But if you are hard on yourself and tell yourself you shouldn't miss him or feel this way, you are just making the grieving process more difficult.

When you are missing your former partner it helps to think about the bad things he did: how bad you felt when you were with him, and what you missed out on because of him. One of the problems when you are in an N relationship is that you aren't acknowledging the reality of the situation. Using this technique helps you put the relationship into perspective when you are just focusing on the good points. If you practice it often enough, you will find your brain automatically shifts from, "I miss him" to "Yeah, but...". Rest assured, you will get to a point where you pity him. It may sound impossible, but it's within your reach! If he is with someone else, just think about what's in store for her!

The angry stage

It's important you do something to release your anger so it doesn't come out later in ways that are destructive or uncontrolled. Withholding your anger can also lead to illness.

I recommend Louise Hay's "Anger Releasing" CD[14]. Another suggestion is to take up an activity which lets you physically release your anger; talking can help, but be careful whom you express these feelings to. You can also write in a journal, paint or take up a new hobby or activity — channel your energy into something positive.

Practice some relaxation therapy

The stress of a relationship break up takes a heavy toll on your body and mind; you need to help yourself cope with this burden by doing something to relax. You will no doubt have your own ways of relaxing, but you may wish to consider some of the following techniques:

❖ Yoga and meditation, even if it's for as little as 10 minutes a day.

❖ Bach flower remedies and essential oils such as lavender, rose, rosemary, jasmine, and neroli.

---

[14] Hay L.L., *Anger releasing,* Hay House, USA, 2004

❖ Reiki and massage treatments to help move the negative energy out of your body when you are most emotional. This helps you move through the grief stages more quickly.

❖ Taking a holiday alone or, if you can't get away, taking some regular time out in your week to pamper yourself.

Getting clear

Make up a vision board listing all the qualities you want in a partner. By being specific about what you want and by focusing your attention on it, you are more likely to attract it to you; although you might see things or people leave your life if they don't match what you are focusing on. For example, within a month of doing her vision board, Sienna found out her partner was cheating, and POOF! He was gone.

The liberating thing about this process is that you don't need to settle for a short list — you can list 100 qualities if you want to! So often women believe that they need to compromise what they want to be in a successful relationship. I believe many women with N partners have this mindset, which is not a bad thing, but it's a paradise for an N because he knows your primary focus is being with him.

In either situation

Trust your intuition

You may find that your body gives you serious warning signs that something is not right.

What to look for:

- ❖ Feeling unhappy unless you are getting positive attention from your N partner

- ❖ Trouble sleeping and eating

- ❖ Inability to concentrate

- ❖ Cocooning (not wanting to go out and do things)

- ❖ Dragging yourself through the day and not having much interest in anything except being with your N partner

- ❖ Body aches and pains

- ❖ Only being interested in things to do with your relationship — relationship self-help books etc.

- ❖ Physical shaking

- ❖ Excessive sweating (a sign your sympathetic nervous system is on overdrive due to stress).

For example, Celia's hands starting shaking uncontrollably when her N husband was near her. A month-and-a-half later he told her he was seeing someone else and left her and their three children for a woman he worked with.

The hand shaking incident was Celia's intuition waving a giant red flag, warning Celia that this man was dangerous to her. She just didn't realise it at the time.

Hone your intuition

Meditate every day, even if it's just for five minutes, and observe situations where you get *déjà vu*-type experiences, feelings about a person or sudden desire to do or not do something that you can't explain. The more you observe and learn from your experiences, you will begin to understand how your intuition works. Also, your friends and family can provide you with insights you might not see because you are in the middle of the situation.

Practice apathy

Any attention, good or bad, is a source of NS[15], so don't give him any sort of reaction. N's don't like to feel they are average, normal or irrelevant, so make them feel that way, and they will stop pressing the buttons that have given them the NS reactions they have been feeding off. They may, however, try new ways of getting a reaction; you need to be prepared for this and practice apathy when they do.

---

[15] Vaknin Dr S., *Toxic Relationships*, p. 139.

A good example is when Carol's ex rang her all upset about his former university classmates (from a decade ago) not paying much attention to him. He had been friendly with them all since leaving university, and saw them every year at an annual get-together. After the most recent function, he complained that he would be out of sight, out of mind for the rest of the year. Carol found it strange that he cared so much about what these people thought of him. What she didn't realise was that he was bemoaning the potential loss of a source of NS: these people were no longer giving him attention and he didn't like it one bit!

Noting this about him, she pretended she didn't even notice her ex if she encountered him in public after their break up. The first time she saw him at a party, she kept her back to him the whole time. He flirted with a group of young women in front of her, but she ignored him. Then he bumped into her and apologised, but Carol didn't turn around. *She gave him nothing.* Carol thought it was hilarious watching him trying to get her attention — "Hey, look at me. LOOK AT MEEE!!! HEY! HEY! I'M OVER HERE!!!"

Break their button

Be aware of the buttons he presses that will get a strong reaction from you — don't give him the satisfaction of seeing it work.

Sarah's N loves it when she gets jealous. One day they were shopping and he commented that if he purchased a certain outfit he would be very popular with the ladies. Sarah decided to "fix his red wagon". She said calmly, "Well, that says a lot about you". She got no answer. She could see him out of the corner of her eye — he was stealing glances at her, watching for the familiar reaction. After a few seconds he said, "Well, it's no fun if you're not going to react!"

Here is a good guide as to what buttons to worry about: focus on something that makes you lose control; or something he keeps doing that upsets you, despite you telling him how you feel about it.

Identify their hook

Narcissists are particularly skilled at what I call "the hook": they know how to get your attention and keep it and they realise they have to win you back after they hurt you.

You need to identify how they "hook" you in. What is it they do that makes you melt into their arms again? If you are going to maintain boundaries with them for bad behaviour, you will need to put up some defenses to their "hook". This is particularly important if you have split up — they will take great delight in being able to reel you in again. "She still wants me after all I did to her. Gee, I still have it!" — are the kinds of things that will be running through his head. Your thoughts are likely to be far more innocent and trusting. Don't become his prey, make him *walk the talk* — if he says he is really sorry for what he did, make him prove it by his actions. Tell him that when you see his actions matching his words you will trust what he says. He won't like it, and is likely to become stroppy and angry. Stand your ground, though; if you don't, he will do the same thing to you over and over again.

For example, Patricia's N decided to offer her a shoulder to cry on when the pastor of their church died. This was three months after telling her he was cheating on her. He was banking on his knight in shining armour act to hook her in again. But it didn't. Patricia had wised up to his tricks and saw it for what it was — an attempt to secure NS.

Get the right support

Trying to deal with an N on your own is tough, lonely and confusing. Knowledge is power, and a good place to start is by taking a look at some of the wonderful online forums and books referred to in the Resources section of this book. I recommend Sam Vaknin's excellent book, "Toxic relationships — abuse and its aftermath", to give you an overview of narcissism and help you gain some control over your situation.

It is helpful, though, having someone to help you piece it all together and work through all the information, which is where therapy is useful. Therapy can also give you practical strategies for coping and a safe place to begin the healing process. If you have battled your feelings alone, you will have someone to help you put the pieces together. A therapist can also help you understand the impact of what you have been through; for instance, you may not realise how exhausting it is putting on a brave face for the rest of the world.

If you are still together, you may benefit from working with a therapist to develop an action plan for dealing with your partner's behaviour.

Make time to be alone

You may find that while you are with an N partner you are so exhausted by the stress and worry that you like being alone a lot. The trick is, though, to ensure you do at least one social thing a week — minimum. If you allow yourself to "disappear" socially, you will find it harder to get back into the social scene later. Isolating yourself may also make you feel worse.

After the break up, friends and family can be well-meaning, but keeping your emotions under control in public can become exhausting. "Keeping busy" can also delay the grieving process and you certainly don't want to dwell there! You need to give yourself plenty of space to go through the grief cycle.

When you are on your own, losing yourself in an activity helps you focus on something other than your N partner and how you are feeling. If you can take your mind off the situation for a minute, then a minute more, you will soon find that you have longer periods where you totally forget about him and the relationship. This is what you are aiming for.

Self-care

Being in a relationship with a narcissist, or surviving one, takes an enormous toll on the body, mind and spirit. To get through this, look after your body. Keep up your serotonin levels with regular exercise, particularly a walk in the early morning sun if you can. Get those endorphins going by watching a comedy each night after work, or reading a funny book. Eat well, and get lots of rest. If you are having trouble sleeping, try taking a cat nap at lunch if possible.

Also, try to spend some time each day in the garden or on a walk; or doing something in the fresh air surrounded by nature to get back into balance.

If you are able to, seek the assistance of a naturopath. Getting the right vitamins and minerals to help your system cope with the stress of your situation can help you cope more successfully and fend off illness caused by the stress you are under.

Journalling in the morning and before bed helps get rid of stress and settle the mind. Don't edit what you write and aim for two pages a day. It helps improve your concentration during the day, as you provide yourself with a guaranteed time to think about the relationship and your feelings.

Another technique you may find helpful is watching movies where people triumph over difficult circumstances or relationship dramas. It can give you a sense that you will be OK too.

What do I want?

You are likely to be spending, or have spent, most of your energy on the relationship and making him happy. So, turn that around! Make a list of things you would like to do today, this week, this month. It doesn't have to be anything major, just something you want for yourself. Take a look at the things you wish he did for you, but doesn't or didn't. Can you do any of those for yourself, or get that need met another way? For example, if he never brings you flowers, you could arrange for flowers to be delivered to your home each week, or pick some up when you do the groceries. Cross things off your list as you do them, it gives you a sense of control that is so lacking when dealing with an N; not to mention it's great for your own development and happiness.

Notice what you enjoy doing and what you get absorbed in. Spending time doing things you are passionate about energises you, puts you in a positive mindset and makes you radiate happiness. When you are in this space you automatically attract positive people and opportunities.

7. What do I say to the therapist?

It is important that you state that you suspect you are in a relationship with a narcissistic partner, and why. It might help to write down what behaviours or traits are troubling you, and think of some examples.

Also work through the list of traits and state how many, and which ones, your partner matches. By doing this preparation you are more likely to get the support that you need.

You also need to get clear about what you want to do. Do you want their help to understand what narcissism is, how it affects you, and work out whether to stay or go? Do you want help to deal with the narcissistic behaviour and stay in the relationship? Or are you looking for support to make the break? If you are unsure, you can always just explain that you are unhappy in the relationship or uncomfortable and you don't know why.

Finding the right therapist

Remember that finding a therapist is like buying the perfect pair of shoes — they need to fit you and be appropriate for the circumstances. So aim for someone who has experience with relationships or dealing with narcissists.

To see how a therapist "fits" you, I recommend calling a few and speaking to them personally about how they work. The aim is to get a sense of what the therapist is like. Do you feel comfortable talking with them? If you feel they are cold or abrupt, would you feel comfortable opening up to them about something as sensitive as this? Trust your instincts and go with the person you "click" with. If you find that the person you picked isn't giving you what you need or want, find someone else. You are giving a lot of power to the therapist at a time when you are vulnerable; you should never feel pressured to keep attending sessions if you don't want to or if you feel uncomfortable for any reason.

Your role

Dealing with your experience is likely to require you to examine your role in the relationship. Why did you allow your partner to treat you this way? It may require some painful self-exploration by going back into your past and dealing with unresolved issues. If you aren't ready for that, focus on how to cope with the current situation — but it's important that you don't rehash what you did, could have, or should have done. Remember, there is no right or wrong way of handling situations — only different choices. Reassure yourself that you did the best you could in the circumstances.

8. Want to have some fun?

I believe that narcissists want control of people and their environment. Given their hypersensitivity to criticism, they are also easily rattled, so if you want to shake their cage a little, here are some tips:

❖ Don't respond to an email, message or text: he'll be calling to see why! If it's so rare to get an email from your N partner that you pounce on it and reply immediately, the change will have him worried. This does not work well, though, if you are generally slack with your responses.

❖ Admire someone else or their achievements: he will have to find fault with them in some way.

❖ If he turns up late or decides he no longer wants to go out, go on your own and don't get back until late. Make sure you are dressed to kill — he will wonder who you are dressing up for! Better still, stay overnight at a friend's place so he has no idea what time you got home!

❖ Cancel a date: he may act indifferent, but it will unsettle him. Then to shake it up even more, be vague about your ability to see him next time: "Mmm, maybe, I'll see what I'm up to and let you know".

❖ Have other plans (that don't include him) when he asks you to attend a work or social function with him: he will have to explain to people where you are, which will embarrass him.

- If he is the type to not make definite plans to see you and just arrive sometime over the weekend, go away for the weekend or out before he usually arrives; and switch off your mobile! He is likely to pretend he doesn't care, but it will worry him.

- Try and get him to confirm a holiday, weekend away or outing in advance and watch him squirm as he tries to avoid it! I believe that many narcissists are also commitment phobic, as they are always on the lookout for a better source of NS. Why commit to plans with you when they might get a better offer from another source?

- Dig deeper: next time he breezes in, get him to talk about the details of what he has been up to. N's often clam up when you start asking questions — they seem to think that sharing details like this makes them less special. Oh please!

- Your partner may discourage you from activities surreptitiously by criticising them or making it difficult for you to attend. For example, he may arrange things at the last minute when he knows your activity is on. What will annoy him no end is to go ahead anyway. If he criticises what you are doing, say breezily, "Oh well, each to their own", and kiss him as you walk out the door. He will be sulking when you get back — openly or privately.

- Get sassy or sassier with him: "What personality am I talking to now?" It will unsettle him, even if he laughs it off.

Please note that you need to be in a position of emotional power to do these things and stick to them. If he still has the power to make you angry, then you are still too close to the situation and may end up getting more hurt when he retaliates. But if you are curious, just try a mild one and see what happens, it can be your little secret. It might even make you feel a little more powerful — he's not the only one that can manipulate!

9. Tips for family and friends

If your loved one is with a narcissistic partner you may have tried, and failed, to bring their attention to problems in their relationship.

This is likely to be because your loved one is confused, ashamed and afraid to deal with the issue. They may have tried to deal with the relationship issues you noticed, but had limited success or a catastrophic failure.

But make no mistake — you are vital to their ability to cope with, leave, and deal with the aftermath of a narcissistic relationship.

What not to do:

❖ *Push:* don't keep telling them all the things you see wrong with the relationship, what you would do, or what they should do. This will only drive them away from you.

❖ *Comment on their partner's absence from social events:* your loved one is already painfully aware of the N's absence and will be dreading having to explain it. They may avoid social situations where they know they will be hounded on this point, which is the worst thing for someone in a relationship with an N to do! They need that external reference point.

❖ *Smother them:* give them space to deal with what they are experiencing.

❖ *If they have broken up, quiz them on why they stayed, why they put up with the behaviour, why they didn't see what was going on*: your loved one is, or was, being emotionally and psychologically abused. Enough said.

Things you can try are:

❖ *Catching up with them regularly*: they may bring up issues in the relationship voluntarily. If they do, that is your chance to gently highlight areas of concern. I would raise them by saying, "How is 'N'?" and let them take it from there.

❖ *Get them out of the house:* your loved one may want to cocoon a lot; they might stay at home and watch a lot of movies, for example. This is one way of coping with the stress of dealing with an N partner, and trying to work out what is happening for themselves. You might want to invite them to an activity you are doing in a group to help them expand their reference point of relationships and people. In this way, you are helping them experience healthy and positive interactions.

❖ *Do things which involve eating healthy food*: many people cannot eat properly (if at all) at times of severe emotional distress. Invite them over for dinner or arrange to have an at-home experimental cooking night where the two of you try out a new recipe. This way they are eating well, learning something new and spending time with you.

❖ *Encourage them to undertake self-care*: things like massages, pedicures etc. If you are able to, try to schedule some sessions together. Just spending time with a friend or relative and not having to talk is very comforting.

❖ *Learn about narcissism*: you might want to mention a fictitious friend who is experiencing narcissistic abuse so your loved one starts asking questions. You could even mention how you are helping this fictitious person through it and the materials you have looked at. This might encourage your friend to look at them in their own time.

Above all — please be gentle. Your loved one is likely to be hiding a great deal of pain, which will impact on their ability to function normally. With your help, though, hopefully they will "see the light" and break free of their situation. Their confidence will already be impacted by the relationship, so coming to terms with the relationship for what it is and leaving will be very difficult. It may take months or years for your loved one to realise what is happening and get the strength to leave.

It takes a special person to give to someone in this situation. Your loved one is lucky to have you!

As the curtains come down on the narcissist's performance, he waits expectantly for rapturous applause and, of course, an encore. But, there is silence. He is shocked to find that his audience is filing out the exits, his girlfriend among them. His girlfriend turns and waves goodbye, smiling at the delicious role reversal that is taking place. For so many years she stood alone, waiting for his attention. Now it is his turn.

10. Resources

Abuse

http://www.enotalone.com/article/4141.html
(An excellent checklist of abusive behaviour.)

http://www.expect-respect.org.nz/thinking.htm
(A list of things to think about in determining if your relationship is abusive. Also look at the excuses tab if you find you are justifying his behaviour!)

http://www.womensaccounts.com/loving_an_abuser_stockholm syndrome.html
(About cognitive dissonance and abusive relationships.)

http://www.abusivelove.com/2006/07/deception-in-abusive-relationships.html

http://en.wikipedia.org/wiki/Cycle_of_abuse
(Geared towards physical abuse, but equally applicable to relationships with narcissists.)

http://www.verbalabuse.com

General

Richardson S., *The Art of Extreme Self Care,* Hay House, USA, 2009

Hicks E. and Hicks J., *The Vortex,* Hay House, USA, 2009

Health

http://www.beyondblue.org.au
(Depression)

http://www.ausflowers.com.au/
(Australian bush flower essences)

Hay L.L., *You can heal your life, Hay House, USA, 2004*

Weil A. M.D., and Leeds J., *Deep Calm*, Sounds True, USA

Narcissism

http://samvak.tripod.com/
(Dr Sam Vaknin's site. You can purchase his books online.
Make this your first stop!)

http://www.abuserecovery.yolasite.com
(An excellent site that looks at who narcissists target, their
tactics, and provides a message forum and comments from
other survivors of narcissistic abuse.)

http://www.narcissismsurvivor.com/resources.html

Narcissist support groups

http://thepsychopath.freeforums.org/

samvak.tripod.com/narclist.html

*http://www.narcissism-abuse-recovery.com/narcissism-support-
group.html*

http://narcissisticpersonalitydisorder.aimoo.com/

http://www.psychforums.com/narcissistic-personality/

Stockholm syndrome

http://www.dailystrength.org/groups/narcissist-victims-syndrome-survivors/discussions/messages/9482876

http://thepsychopath.freeforums.org/why-do-i-keep-going-back-for-more-abuse-t11756.html

I welcome your comments about this book and your suggestions for future editions.

Contact: whatiswrongwithmyrelationship@gmail.com